All About YOU

Quiz Book

Discover more about
yourself and how
to be your best!

by Dr. Lynda Madison
illustrated by Shannon Laskey

★ American Girl®

Editorial Development: Erin Falligant
Design and Art Direction: Chris Lorette David
Production: Sarah Boecher, Judith Lary, Jeannette Bailey
Illustrations: Shannon Laskey

Dear Reader,

Are you outgoing? Organized? Free-spirited? Do you know all the roles you play in your family and on the teams you join?

The way you act and the things you like give clues about your personal style. The quizzes in this book will reveal lots of fun and interesting discoveries about who you are. You'll also find hints to help things go smoothly—with your friends, your family, your classmates, and your team.

Ready to get started? Grab a pencil, and find out what your answers to these quizzes say about **you!**

Your friends at American Girl

Friends

What kind of friend do you tend to be? Are you trustworthy? Thoughtful? Brave? Find out how you can be an even better buddy—to others and to *yourself*.

What's Your Social Style?

Some people are always surrounded by a group of friends. Other people stick close to only a few. What does your friendship circle look like, and what does it say about you?

1. You're upset about something a girl said at school, and you need some advice. You're most likely to . . .

    a. talk to Mom or Dad over dinner.

    b. grab the phone to call a good friend.

    c. tell your story to the kids on the bus and ask them, "What should I do?!"

2. It's Saturday night, and you're bored. You're most likely to . . .

    a. turn on a movie to watch with your sister.

    b. invite your best friend for a sleepover.

    c. ask your parents if they'll take you and some friends mini golfing.

3. Your mom says you can invite a friend to a movie, but at the last minute your friend can't come. You . . .

   a. go ahead with your family. Maybe your friend can come another time.

   b. check with another friend before going with your family.

   c. call everyone you know until you find someone who can go.

4. Your parents are going out of town for the night and you need a place to stay. You'd most like to . . .

   a. stay with your favorite aunt.

   b. sleep at a friend's house.

   c. go to a slumber party.

5. Most of your friends are from . . .

   a. school only.

   b. school and an activity you are in, such as dance or soccer or swim team.

   c. anywhere you can find them. You make friends wherever you go.

Answers

Mostly a's

You can count on your family to be there for you, which is great! To make more friends outside your family, ask someone new to sit with you at lunch. Or join an activity, such as Girl Scouts or karate, for a chance to meet new people.

Mostly b's

You stick close to a good friend or two rather than gathering with a crowd. Having a few special people you can rely on is important, but make time and room for other people, too. It's easy for jealousies to start when a group is too small or tight-knit. And there are so many people to know and to like!

Mostly c's

You love having a swirl of people around you. Gathering with groups can be fun, but don't get *too* caught up in the action. Also, plan one-on-one time with friends, so that you can really get to know each other and stay connected. And don't forget to make time for family.

It's All About Trust

Trust is an important part of any relationship. Your friends need to be able to count on you to do what you say and say what you mean. How high is your Trust Tally?

1. Your friend tells you she likes a boy. She doesn't say it's a secret, but you ask her permission anyway before you tell anyone else.

☐ **Sounds like you**   ☐ **Nope, not you**

2. You tell your friend you will go with her to a sleepover this weekend because she doesn't want to go alone. But on Friday, you say, "I don't really want to go. Maybe you can find someone else."

☐ **Sounds like you**   ☐ **Nope, not you**

3. Your friend asks your honest opinion about a shirt that you think looks awful on her. You say, "I don't think it's your best style. But I *love* the blue one on you."

☐ **Sounds like you**   ☐ **Nope, not you**

4. A girl at your lunch table says something untrue about your friend, who isn't there to defend herself. You take a deep breath and say, "Actually, I know her, and she's not like that at all."

☐ **Sounds like you**   ☐ **Nope, not you**

5. Your best friend tells you she's moving out of town and asks you to keep it a secret. You tell another friend but make her promise not to tell anyone else.

☐ **Sounds like you**   ☐ **Nope, not you**

Answers

☐ **Mostly blue**

Your Trust Tally is high. Your friends can count on you to respect their feelings and their secrets. When you're honest and follow through on promises, you set the stage for a long-lasting friendship.

☐ **Mostly green**

You might need to put yourself in your friends' shoes. How would you want a friend to act in each of these situations? To boost your Trust Tally, treat others the way you'd like to be treated.

Big Important Point

Some things your friends share with you should be kept private even if your friends don't call them "secrets." Not sure whether to zip your lips? Ask yourself these questions:

- **Would the friend who told you be happy if you told other people?**

- **Might others be hurtful to your friend if they knew?**

- **Would you want other people to know if this were your secret?**

- **Would your friend trust you again if you told?**

If your answer to any of these questions is "no," don't let the secret out. You should tell someone only if you think something bad could happen to your friend if you don't tell. In that case, share the secret with a parent or another adult you trust, who can help you decide what to do next.

Who's in Charge?

Sometimes other people want us to do things that we don't think we should do. Do you go along with the crowd, or stay true to yourself? Take this quiz to find out.

1. A friend in another class already took the test you're about to take. She asks, "Want to see the right answers?"

☐ **do it**　**or**　☐ **don't do it**

2. You got sick the last two times you rode the Twirler at the fair. You want to step out of the line, but the kids you're with are calling you a scaredy-cat.

☐ **ride it**　**or**　☐ **don't ride it**

3. Your teacher said to watch the news for the answer to a bonus quiz question. Your classmates didn't watch. They beg you to tell them the answer.

☐ **do it**　**or**　☐ **don't do it**

4. Some friends want you to swim in a pool when the lifeguard's not there. "Don't worry. It'll be fine," they say.

☐ **do it**   or   ☐ **don't do it**

5. You like to watch soccer, but joining the team is just not for you. "Do it for us," your friends beg you.

☐ **do it**   or   ☐ **don't do it**

Answers

If you answered **"don't"** most often, you know your own mind and aren't afraid to tell others where you stand. If you need help finding your voice, try these tips:

1. **Be honest.** You won't feel good about any grades you earn by cheating. If people pressure you to cheat, just say, "Thanks, but I want to see how I do on my own."

2. **Be smart.** Don't do anything that has made you sick in the past. Simply tell your friends, "I think I'll sit this one out." There's no shame in knowing your own limits.

3. **Be brave.** If you did an assignment and your friends didn't, don't hand it over to them. Say, "I'd rather not. I worked hard for this."

4. **Be safe.** Swimming is safe only when a lifeguard is watching. What if one of your friends isn't a strong swimmer and needs help? It's dangerous to take chances just because it sounds fun.

5. **Be true to yourself.** If your friends want you to join them in a sport you don't enjoy, cheer them on from the sidelines, or spend that time doing something that *you* love.

Standing Up for Others

What do you do when a friend is in need? Can you stand up to others to help someone else?

1. A girl in your class invites all the girls to join her club—except your best friend. You . . .

    a. secretly join the club, sad that your friend will be left out.

    b. tell your friend that if she can't join, you won't either.

    c. say to the club leader, "I'm sorry, but I won't join a club that leaves people out."

2. You see the new girl in school standing alone in the cafeteria, not sure where to sit. You . . .

    a. hope for her sake she finds a spot soon.

    b. ask your friends, "Do you mind if she sits here?"

    c. wave to her and ask, "Would you like to eat with us?"

3. Your friend got her hair cut, and kids are laughing because it's so short. You . . .

   a. pull your friend aside and say, "Don't worry. It'll grow back."

   b. call attention to your own hair, hoping the kids will tease you instead.

   c. say to them, "Hey, that's pretty mean."

4. On the playground some kids are choosing teams for a relay race. Riley isn't very fast, but you hate to see her get chosen last, again. You . . .

   a. cross your fingers and hope someone chooses her.

   b. say to the captain, "Riley needs a team!"

   c. jump in as a captain for the next race so that you can choose Riley first.

5. A friend has a serious problem with someone who is being mean to her, and she comes to you for advice. You . . .

   a. tell her you hope things get better, but you're not sure how you can help.

   b. say, "That's a tough situation. Do you think you should talk to a grown-up?"

   c. offer to go with her to talk to a school counselor about the problem.

Answers

Mostly a's

You care how others feel but are sometimes afraid to say what's on your mind. It's not easy, but try harder to speak up. Every time you stand up for someone else, you'll feel stronger and better about yourself, too.

Mostly b's

Friends and classmates can count on you to be in their corner. Keep up the kindness, and don't be afraid to let others know if they're acting in an unkind way. When you speak up, chances are good that you'll find some people standing beside you.

Mostly c's

You know what you believe and have no trouble standing up for others. People probably rely on you to do the right thing. By taking action and being a leader, you're showing other people how to help, too.

Family

Did you ever think about the ways you fit into your family? Or about what makes you stand out? You can learn a lot about yourself from the people closest to you, and there's always more you can learn about *them*, too.

Same or Different?

You know what you like. Are there others in your family who like the same things? Take this quiz with a parent, a sibling, or another relative. You might be surprised by what you have in common!

Me

Would you rather . . .

Ride a horse ☑ or ☐ Ride a bicycle

Read a magazine ☐ or ☑ Read a book

Fly a kite ☑ or ☐ Fly a plane

Talk to a movie star ☑ or ☐ Talk to the President

Sleep in a tent ☑ or ☐ Sleep in a cabin

Eat pizza ☐ or ☑ Eat spaghetti

Watch a movie at home ☑ or ☐ Watch a movie in a theater

Play a video game ☐ or ☑ Play a card game

Walk in the mall ☑ or ☐ Walk in the woods

Sing on a stage ☑ or ☐ Sing in the shower

Wear a skirt ☑ or ☐ Wear shorts

Win a trip ☑ or ☐ Win a computer

My Relative

Would you rather . . .

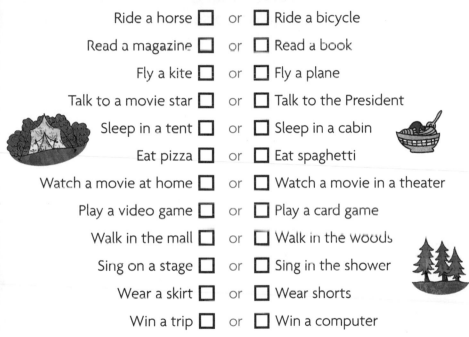

Ride a horse ☐ or ☐ Ride a bicycle

Read a magazine ☐ or ☐ Read a book

Fly a kite ☐ or ☐ Fly a plane

Talk to a movie star ☐ or ☐ Talk to the President

Sleep in a tent ☐ or ☐ Sleep in a cabin

Eat pizza ☐ or ☐ Eat spaghetti

Watch a movie at home ☐ or ☐ Watch a movie in a theater

Play a video game ☐ or ☐ Play a card game

Walk in the mall ☐ or ☐ Walk in the woods

Sing on a stage ☐ or ☐ Sing in the shower

Wear a skirt ☐ or ☐ Wear shorts

Win a trip ☐ or ☐ Win a computer

Big important point: If you think you have nothing in common with a family member, maybe you just haven't asked the right questions. Get the conversation started the next time you're sitting around the dinner table or riding in the car.

The Roles You Play

Check all the statements below that describe something you might do. Then count the colors to see which family roles describe you!

☐ Your parents disagree about who was supposed to have picked up dinner after work. You say, "It's O.K. Maybe we have a pizza in the freezer."

☐ Your brother had a bad day at school and is stomping around the house. You stomp around, too, trying to get him to laugh.

☐ It seems as if nothing's planned for the evening—again. You gather everyone in the living room and pull out the board games.

☐ No one seems to care where the family goes to dinner, but you do. You insist on your favorite restaurant.

☐ You win a T-shirt in a school raffle. Your sister is sad because she's never won anything, so you hand the shirt over to her.

☐ It's raining and dreary and the family's moping around. You say, "Who needs sunshine? Let's have an indoor picnic!"

☐ Your siblings start to argue about who sat where at dinner last night. You tell them exactly where they should sit. After all, when you're right, you're right.

☐ In a hotel room at night, your silly comments keep everyone awake—and laughing.

How many of each color did you check? If you checked two of any color, turn the page to find a role you may play in your family.

_____ ☐   _____ ☐

_____ ☐   _____ ☐

Answers

2 ☐s

You like things to be calm in your household, and you work hard to keep other people happy. It's great that you care about people's feelings. Just be sure that you aren't keeping your own feelings bottled up inside.

2 ☐s

You are confident and assertive and know how to make things happen. This probably helps keep your family organized. But while you're moving things along, be careful to consider other people's feelings. They may have a harder time speaking up than you, and their opinions count, too.

2 ☐s

You like to make things fun for your family. Your cheerful nature is a gift. Remember to ask family members for their ideas, too, before you jump right into the next activity on your list.

2 ☐s

You enjoy making others laugh and are often the life of the party. Just be sure you know when to stop. There's a time to be funny and a time to be serious.

Friends in the Family

Having siblings is the most fun when you feel as if you're *friends*, too. Take this quiz to see how "friendly" you are to your sibs.

1. Your sister got into trouble at school this morning because she forgot her homework. You . . .

   a. say, "Again?! Your grades must be terrible!"

   b. can tell she's feeling frustrated, so you promise to help her remember her homework tomorrow.

2. You have swim class after school, but your brother missed his bus home. He will have to wait a long time for your mom to come for both of you. You . . .

a. tell him, "Deal with it. You'll just have to wait."

b. invite him to time your laps. Maybe he'll get interested in swimming, too.

3. Your sister lost a bracelet that belonged to your mom. You . . .

a. breathe a sigh of relief. You're just glad it wasn't something of yours.

b. say, "Hmm . . . where did you see it last? Come on. I'll help you look for it."

4. Your little brother bugs you and your friend to let him play ball with you. You say . . .

a. "Why don't you go find your own friends?"

b. "Sure, you can play with us for a while."

5. Your little sister can't sleep after watching a movie you thought was funny, not scary. You . . .

a. poke fun at her with a scary noise or two.

b. remind her that it was just pretend and try to get her talking about something else.

Answers

Mostly a's

You like to stay out of your siblings' business, but try not to be mean about it. When your brother or sister has a problem, take a moment to understand how it feels. You'd appreciate that if you were in a similar situation—and when you *are*, your sibs will be more likely to be there for you.

Mostly b's

You like to take care of your siblings and help them solve problems, which is what a great sister does. You don't have to do everything for your sibs all the time—that could wear you out. But listening and making a kind suggestion can go a long way toward keeping things friendly and happy at your house.

Do You Put Up or Speak Up?

Do you shout out your point of view when things don't go your way at home? Or do you keep your thoughts to yourself and hope the problem goes away? Circle your answers below to learn more about how you handle conflict.

1. You asked your dad for a hot dog, but he grilled you a hamburger instead. You . . .

    a. say, "Hey, no fair. Where's my hot dog?!"

    b. say, "I was hoping for a hot dog, Dad. Are there any left?"

    c. eat what he served you and keep your complaints to yourself.

2. Just to bug you, your brother repeats everything you say, right after you say it. It goes on and on and on. You . . .

    a. shout, "Quit being such a baby!" (which he repeats back to you).

    b. say, "Why don't we play a game?" After all, he just wants your attention.

    c. ignore him until he moves on to something else.

3. You helped sort laundry this morning, but when you ask to have a friend over, your mom says she wants help folding towels. You . . .

   a. stomp off, saying, "That's not fair! I was helping all morning!"

   b. ask, "Can Jill come for a little while if I fold towels right away?"

   c. sulk in your room because you never get your way.

4. Your brother's playing games on the computer, and you need to look something up for a report you are writing. You . . .

   a. say, "Get off! I have important homework to do."

   b. ask, "Can I get on for five minutes to look up a question?"

   c. walk past him a couple of times and sigh loudly, hoping he'll get the hint.

5. For your mother's birthday, your sister bought a picture frame—which was what *you* were going to get your mom. You . . .

   a. tell your sister she stole your idea and has to return the picture frame.

   b. say, "How about I pay for half? Then it can be from both of us."

   c. get a frame of your own for your mom. You hope she'll be happy with two.

Answers

Mostly a's

You are quick to let others know how you feel, but watch how you say things. If you ask politely for what you need, you won't hurt others' feelings. And you'll be more likely to get what you want.

Mostly b's

You are assertive and know how to compromise. When you ask calmly or suggest a solution, you and your family get more of what you need. Just be sure to stay calm if someone turns you down. You can always try again later.

Mostly c's

You know how you feel but tend to keep it to yourself. Be careful. You may get taken advantage of if you don't speak up. Practice telling others what you want so that they can give a little, too.

Three Tips for Saying How You Feel

- Start your sentences with the word *I* instead of the word *You*. That way others won't feel as if you're blaming them. Say,

I feel hurt. or "I feel angry." Keep a list of feeling words handy to help you describe your emotions.

Sad	Angry	Nervous
Unheard	Shy	Fearful
Misunderstood		Scared
Envious		Disrespected
Tired	Hurt	Mistreated
Worried		Embarrassed
Jealous	Annoyed	Sorry
Guilty	Confused	Ashamed

- Be specific about *when* and *why* you feel that way, such as "I feel sad when I am left out."

- Say what you think might help you feel better, such as "I'd appreciate it if you would include me next time," or "I'd feel less _____ if we did things this way." When people know how you feel and how they can help, they are more likely to meet your needs.

School

Are you a planner or a procrastinator? What's your favorite role in a group project? And how do you learn best? Pick up your pencil, because these pop quizzes are all about you.

Backpacking Clues

The things you put in and on your backpack can give hints about your personal style. Take this quiz to find out what the pack on your back says about you.

Check the box by every item you find IN your backpack:

Homework assignments . . . . ☐

Colored pens or pencils . . . . ☐

More than two schoolbooks. . . . . ☐

A novel or magazine . . . . ☐

Something from a club or activity . . . . ☐

A calculator . . . . ☐

Pens with blue or black ink . . . . ☐

Notes from friends . . . . ☐

A drawing or poem . . . . ☐

Check the box by each thing you put ON your backpack:

Flowers or doodles . . . . ☐

Buttons or pins . . . . ☐

A school sticker . . . . ☐

Words you wrote. . . . . ☐

A smiley face . . . . ☐

A sports team slogan . . . . ☐

A tag or ID saying "Property of ___" . . . ☐

Something a friend gave you . . . . ☐

Ribbons or beads . . . . ☐

PROPERTY OF
Moi!

Answers

How many of each color did you check?

_____ ☐   _____ ☐   _____ ☐

3 or more ☐

You are upbeat and love to be with friends. School spirit just might be one of your strengths.

3 or more ☐

Your backpack says that you take school seriously. You are prepared for your classes and ready to go for the grades.

3 or more ☐

All your doodads and doodling tell others that you are creative and bring your own style to the things you do at school.

How Do You Like to Learn?

Everyone learns by seeing, hearing, and doing things. Do you like one way of learning better than the others? Take this quiz to find out. Circle the answer that sounds like what you'd do.

1. Your friend tries to tell you how to get to her house. You . . .

    a. say the directions back to her, to be sure you heard right.

    b. ask her to draw you a map.

    c. ask if you can ride home with her the first time or two.

2. You need to memorize your lines for the school play. You . . .

    a. say the lines out loud in front of a mirror.

    b. carry the script in your backpack and read your lines over and over.

    c. invite a friend over to help you act out your scenes.

3. Your class takes a field trip to the zoo to learn more about lions. You . . .

    a. listen to the audio recording through the headphones by the cage.

    b. check out the signs on the walls to see where the lions came from.

    c. imitate the lions as they lick their paws and wash their faces.

4. You want to remember the steps to a new dance routine. You . . .

    a. get a CD of the music so that you can play it at home.

    b. ask your dance teacher to show you the steps again.

    c. practice the routine every night with your sister.

5. You hope to learn a few more words in Spanish. You . . .

    a. listen to the Spanish channel on TV.

    b. look up the words in an online language dictionary.

    c. practice saying the words to your neighbor, who speaks Spanish.

Answers

Mostly a's

You like to learn by **hearing** information. Repeating numbers, words, or facts out loud can help you remember them better. Even saying things silently to yourself (in your head) will help the information stick.

Mostly b's

You like to **see** the things you are trying to learn. Pictures, charts, and graphs are your favorite study aids. To remember them even better, try closing your eyes and imagining the words and pictures again in your mind.

Mostly c's

You like to learn by taking action and **doing** the work. Acting things out or imagining yourself doing them is a great way to help yourself remember.

Most people learn best through a combination of ways. Be creative about how you study. You'll have a better shot at remembering information, and you'll have a lot more fun, too!

Planner or Procrastinator?

Do you put off homework and chores? Or do you charge ahead to get the job done? Circle the answers below that sound like something you'd do.

1. Your teacher assigns a research paper that's due in a month. You . . .

    a. choose a topic quickly and plan to do a little bit each week so that you're sure to have it all done by the deadline.

    b. figure your teacher will tell you when you need to do the next part. Why worry about it now?

2. You have a spelling test coming up at the end of the week. You . . .

    a. start looking at the words today so that you'll have time to memorize the ones you don't know.

    b. remember about the test the night before. You frantically search your backpack for the list of words, but it's nowhere to be found!

3. You know you have chores to do before you can go to your friend's birthday party. You . . .

    a. get up early to start so that you're sure to get them done.

    b. start a half hour before the party. When you run out of time, you beg your parents to let you finish them tomorrow.

4. You need to memorize a poem to recite out loud. You . . .

    a. talk your brother into reading the lines with you over breakfast each morning. By the end of the week, you both know them by heart.

    b. try to memorize the lines while watching your favorite TV show, but there just aren't enough commercial breaks.

5. It's late, and you're tired. Your mom says, "Get to bed. You have school tomorrow." You . . .

    a. brush your teeth and hop in. You do your best with a good night's sleep.

    b. say, "But, Mom! I haven't even started my homework yet!"

Answers

If you answered mostly **a's**, you plan ahead to meet your goals. When a big project looms, you're sure to get the job done. If you answered mostly **b's**, procrastination is slowing you down. Follow these tips to put more planning into your projects:

- **Start today.** If you have chores or assignments to do, start as soon as you can. You can't finish what you don't start!
- **Break it down.** Separate big projects into smaller parts, and do them one at a time.
- **Record it.** Mark all your assignments on a calendar, and check it each day to know what's due when.
- **Practice it.** To learn something well, practice it a little each day rather than trying to cram it into your brain all at once. You'll remember it better that way.
- **Reward yourself.** Plan to do something fun when your work is done—and *only* when it's done. You'll work harder that way.

Team Player

Working on a group presentation or science project? This quiz gives you clues about the skills you bring to your team projects.

Your group's assignment is "The Life Cycle of Bees." Check each sentence that sounds like something you might say in your group:

☐ "I found some markers we can use for our poster!"

☐ "We should write down what we'll each say and do."

☐ "I found a quote for our poster. Here, listen to this . . ."

☐ "I wrote a poem called 'Bees, If You Please.' Want to hear it?"

- ☐ "Look at this chart I made on my computer."

- ☐ "How long do bees live?"

- ☐ "In the dictionary, *migrate* means 'to move somewhere else.'"

- ☐ "This paragraph about honey is way too long."

- ☐ "I drew some bees. Want to see?"

- ☐ "How long will it take you to finish the poster?"

- ☐ "Listen to this article I found about queen bees."

- ☐ "What do you guys think our title should be?"

- ☐ "I think a honeycomb background would look great on our poster!"

- ☐ "I'll find out if we can present our project first."

- ☐ "This book says up to 1,000 bees can live in one hive!"

- ☐ "There's a typo in the paragraph where we talk about hives."

Answers

Did you check two or more sentences of any one color? If so, find that color below to see what it means about how you work with your team.

☐ Designer

You like to make projects look great by adding drawings, photos, and charts that you create.

☐ Team Leader

You tend to take charge and keep things on track. With an eye on the deadline, you make sure things get done.

☐ Fact Finder

Whether you're surfing online or flipping through the pages of a book, you enjoy finding fun facts that make your project more interesting.

☐ Writer/Editor

You enjoy writing about your topic and making sure things are said clearly so that others understand what your project is all about.

Top Tips for Teams

Whether your team is in the classroom or on a soccer field, you'll want to help keep team spirit high. Here's how:

- Tell others what they are doing right, not wrong. Then make suggestions you think will help things go even better.

- Talk privately with anyone who you think could do more, rather than complaining to the rest of the team. Remember, your teacher or coach probably knows who works hard and who doesn't.

- Know that other people won't do things exactly as you would. Everyone brings different skills to the group.

FUN & GAMES

Would you rather play a board game, a basketball game, or a video game? And what kinds of things tickle your funny bone? When it comes to the ways you spend your free time, you are uniquely you.

The Ways You Play

Check the **top five** activities that you would enjoy most if you had the chance. Then find out what those hobbies say about you.

In my spare time, I might . . .

☐ put seashells or stones in a bag to save.

☐ draw pictures.

☑ play a video game.

☑ shoot baskets.

☐ organize my state coins.

☐ make up songs.

☐ dance to music.

☐ challenge my sister at checkers.

☐ line shelves with my duck knickknacks.

☐ write a story.

☑ dig out my board games.

☐ make up a gymnastics routine.

☐ sort my CDs or movies.

☐ bead a bracelet.

☐ play games on my favorite Web site.

☑ time myself running around the yard.

☐ buy more trading cards.

☑ take photos of my dog.

☐ find someone to play cards with.

☐ gather neighbor kids for a soccer game.

Answers

2 or more ☐

Collecting groups of things is one of *your* main things. You may have lots of different collections. Knowing what you like makes it fun to scout for more. It can give other people hints, too, when they're looking for the right gift for you.

2 or more ☐

You like to create things you can show to your friends or just enjoy on your own. You can probably be found in a craft store now and then, looking for new ways to make and display your artwork.

2 or more ☐

Games are the thing for you. You love figuring out strategies and competing with yourself or with others. You might even have fun making up some games of your own!

2 or more ☐

Putting forth a little physical effort is one of your favorite pastimes, and you're likely to be involved in at least one sport. You enjoy being active, which is good for your body and your mind.

How Adventurous Are You?

Do you tiptoe around the action or do you dive right in? Take this quiz to find out.

1. It's pouring outside and the puddles are filling. You . . .

   a. yell, "It's raining! Let's go!" and run for the water without even rolling up your pant legs.

   b. ask a parent if it's O.K., and then dance in the raindrops.

   c. hand your sister an umbrella and say, "Have a good time."

2. At the amusement park, your friends all dash for the Super Shaker ride. You . . .

   a. grab a seat, too, ready for a thrill.

   b. ask, "Has anyone ever been on that?" before you decide if you're going.

   c. sit down on a bench. No way are you riding.

3. A farm in the country advertises a life-size maze made out of hay bales. Your parents buy tickets for your whole family to go. You . . .

    a. disappear into the maze, yelling, "Don't get lost, anyone!"

    b. say, "Let's all stay together," and keep your parents in sight.

    c. grab someone's hand to make sure you're not alone in there.

4. At summer camp, the kids split up and head off for different activities. You . . .

    a. shout, "I'm doing the mud slide."

    b. ask, "Does anyone want to swim with me?"

    c. sit down on a tree stump, not sure what to choose.

5. Your friend invites you to ride the go-carts. You . . .

    a. press the pedal to the floor, yelling, "Whoo-hoo!" as you buzz by her.

    b. keep a slow and steady pace, staying a safe distance from the other carts.

    c. say, "If I'm going, you're driving!"

Answers

Mostly a's

You dive right in. You love to find the fun in things and will fling yourself into any challenge. Trouble is, you could get hurt if you rush in too quickly or don't wait for instructions. Always be sure to check out the risks before you charge ahead.

Mostly b's

You approach activities with caution. Sure, you love having fun as much as your friends do, but you think things through a little, too. That's a good habit to have. You balance your sense of adventure with a helpful dose of common sense.

Mostly c's

You watch and wait. You might enjoy adventurous things if you gave them a try, but your cautious nature may be holding you back. Consider stretching yourself just a little and trying something new. You may have more fun than you think you will!

Are You a Super Sport?

How do you handle winning, losing, and everything in between? Add up your Super Sport Score by circling what you would do in each situation.

1. Your friends are at your house, and you're winning at your own video game. You know you should let someone else play, but you don't want to quit. You . . .

   a. stop your game after ten minutes and let your friends take a turn.

   b. say, "Hold on, everyone. I'm about to score again!"

2. Your soccer team loses the fourth game in a row. You . . .

   a. tell your team, "We'll do better next week. We just need more practice."

   b. say, "That ref needs glasses. No way did that team's goal count."

3. You lose at Crazy Eights, which you played only because your sister begged you to. You . . .

   a. tell her, "You're good at this. I can tell you've played a lot."

   b. say, "What a dumb game. You won by sheer luck."

4. Your team just won! They go wild, yelling, "We're the best!" right at the other team. You . . .

   a. shake hands with the other team's players, then whoop it up on your own end of the field.

   b. yell right along with your teammates. You deserve to celebrate, don't you?

5. Your coach doesn't seem to let you play as often as your teammates. You . . .

   a. ask your coach for pointers. If he sees that you want to get better, maybe he'll put you in the game more often so that you can practice.

   b. complain to your teammates, saying, "I don't think he likes me at all."

If you answered mostly **a's**, you're a super-good sport—and a winner no matter what the scoreboard says. If you answered mostly **b's**, you may need more practice keeping your cool. Try these tips:

1. **Share the glory.** Winning feels great, but it feels even better when your friends are winning right along with you. Take turns and support one another.
2. **Respect rules and referees.** Most of the time, refs can see things you can't see while you're playing the game.
3. **Be a role model.** When you lose, be the first one to congratulate the other team. Then focus on all the things your team did well.
4. **Celebrate later.** When you win, hold off on whooping it up until after you shake hands with the other person or team.
5. **Speak up.** If you want more playing time, let your coach know—and be prepared to follow through on any suggestions your coach has for you.

What Tickles Your Funny Bone?

You love to laugh. Everybody does! Take this quiz to find out more about how you clown around.

Check off each statement below that sounds like something you'd do.

☐ You're sitting with friends when someone pops a balloon. You fall out of your chair and pretend to run for cover.

☐ You make a card for a friend with a picture of a frog on it. The card says, "Have a Hoppy Day."

☐ You think it's a hoot when you set your sister's clock ahead and she gets up an hour early for school.

☐ In the school cafeteria, you burst out with a quote from your favorite movie. You sound just like the lead character.

☐ At a party, you get everyone's attention so that you can tell your latest "Why did the chicken cross the road?" joke.

☐ You laugh with glee when your father can't get salt from the shaker because you put plastic wrap under the lid.

☐ From behind the kitchen counter, you call, "Look, everyone!" You crouch lower as you walk, so it looks as if you're going down stairs.

☐ You laugh when you see "jumbo shrimp" on a menu. It doesn't make sense that something shrimpy could be jumbo, too.

☐ You tell the whole class to sit in different seats today, just to see how your favorite teacher reacts.

☐ At the dinner table, you say, "Hey, watch this." You just discovered you can wiggle your ears!

☐ You giggle when you see a bumper sticker that reads, "Honk if you love peace and quiet."

☐ On your mother's birthday, you wrap her necklace in a box, inside another box, inside another box. It's fun to watch her face as she opens each one.

Answers

☐ Mostly green

You love making people laugh, and you're probably the life of the party. Just make sure you know when it's O.K. to clown around. Even if you get a big laugh, take a few seconds to look around. Did you interrupt something that someone was trying to say or do? If so, settle down. There might be a better time to act silly.

☐ Mostly blue

You can't wait for April Fool's Day—you *love* playing tricks on your friends. Before you open your bag of tricks, make sure those practical jokes won't harm anyone or anything. And ask yourself if the person you're tricking will think it's funny or might get mad. Save pranks for the friends you know well, the ones who think your jokes are just as fun and funny as you do.

☐ Mostly red

Words are your thing, and you use them to get laughs. Those laughs will keep on coming as long as you make sure your comments are always as kind as they are clever.

Tied to Technology?

Are you a girl who loves gadgets—video games, computers, MP3 players, and more? Check your choices below to see how much you tune in to technology.

Which would you rather do?

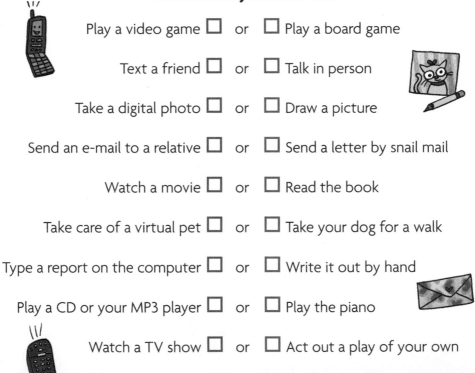

Play a video game ☐ or ☐ Play a board game

Text a friend ☐ or ☐ Talk in person

Take a digital photo ☐ or ☐ Draw a picture

Send an e-mail to a relative ☐ or ☐ Send a letter by snail mail

Watch a movie ☐ or ☐ Read the book

Take care of a virtual pet ☐ or ☐ Take your dog for a walk

Type a report on the computer ☐ or ☐ Write it out by hand

Play a CD or your MP3 player ☐ or ☐ Play the piano

Watch a TV show ☐ or ☐ Act out a play of your own

Answers

☐ **Mostly blue**

You may love to surf the Web, e-mail your friends, or play video games. Just be sure you set aside your gadgets for some face-to-face time with people, too. That's the best way to stay connected to your family and friends.

☐ **Mostly green**

You have found a way to balance technology with some off-line activities. Good for you! When you aren't online all the time or using some gadget, you are more likely to be talking with friends and family—and staying active.

What did you learn from the quizzes in this book? Did you discover any traits or talents you never knew you had? When you know what makes you unique, you're a happier and more confident girl. Tear out the cootie-catcher quizzes at the back of this book to learn more about what makes your friends and family special, too.

☑ happy

☑ confident

☑ special

Write to us!

Tell us what you learned about yourself. Send letters to:

All About You Quiz Book Editor
American Girl
8400 Fairway Place
Middleton, WI, 53562

(All comments and suggestions received by American GIrl may be used without
compensation or acknowledgment. Sorry—photos can't be returned.)

Here are some other American Girl books you might like:

❑ I read it.

❑ I read it.

❑ I read it.

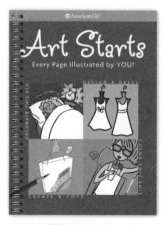

❑ I read it.

Cootie Catcher Instructions

1. Tear out one cootie catcher. Fold and unfold it in half diagonally in both directions to make an X. Place the square picture-side down.

2. Fold each corner point into the center.

3. Flip so that flaps are facedown. Then fold each corner into the center.

4. Fold in half this way to crease.

5. Then unfold and fold in half the other way.

Put your pointer fingers in the back pockets.

Put your thumbs in the front pockets.

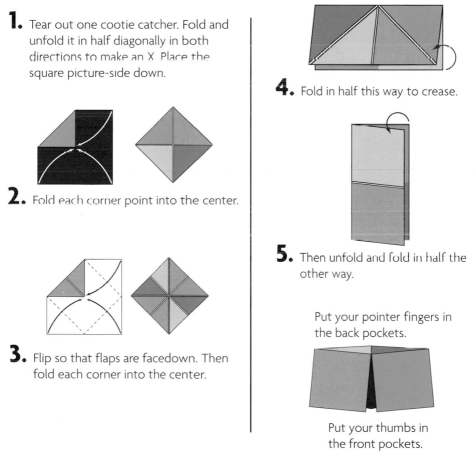

How to Play

1. Insert your pointer fingers and thumbs under the numbered flaps on the cootie catcher.

2. Ask a friend or family member to choose a number from one of the outside flaps. Open and close your fingers that number of times, moving your fingers front to back and then sideways.

3. Have your friend choose a word from the inside of the cootie catcher. Spell out the word, opening and closing your fingers with each letter.

4. Have your friend pick one of the words that shows. Open that flap and read the question beneath. Have your friend answer the question. Take turns so that you can answer a question, too!

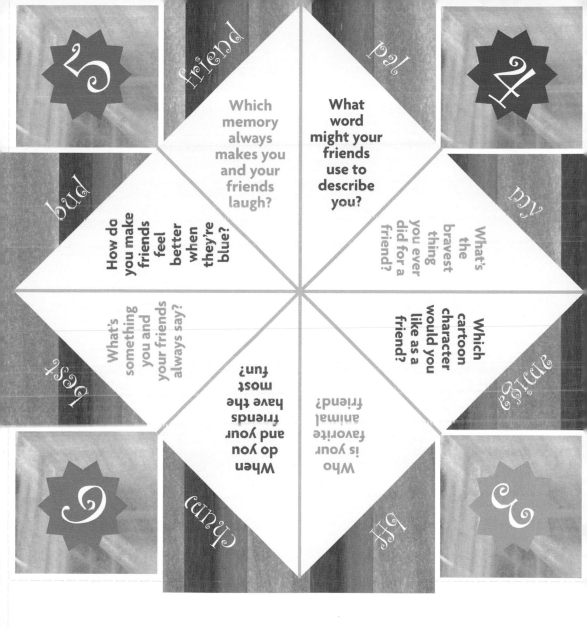

5

4

friend

pal

bud

my

best

amigo

6

3

chum

bff

Which memory always makes you and your friends laugh?

What word might your friends use to describe you?

How do you make friends feel better when they're blue?

What's the bravest thing you ever did for a friend?

What's something you and your friends always say?

Which cartoon character would you like as a friend?

When do you and your friends have the most fun?

Who is your favorite animal friend?

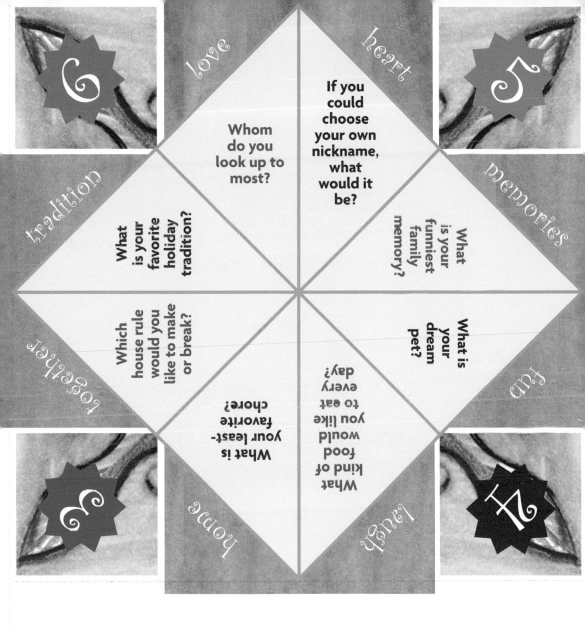

6

3

think

discover

why not

wonder

What is your dream job?

Which foreign language would you like to speak well?

If you could be any character in a book, which one would you be?

If you were a teacher, which subject would you like to teach?

learn

share

grow

why

What was your most embarrassing moment at school?

Which hot lunch could you eat every single day?

Which planet would you like to visit?

If you were in charge at school, what's one thing you would change?

5

4